Secrets of Forex Trading

A Beginner's Guide To Forex Trading

Robert Hill

Published by Dr. Patrick Johnson, 2022.

While every precaution has been taken in the preparation of this book, the publisher assumes no responsibility for errors or omissions, or for damages resulting from the use of the information contained herein.

Secrets of Forex Trading- A Beginner's Guide To Forex Trading

First Edition. December 2022.

Table of Contents

Legal Notices & Disclaimers

Introduction

The largest foreign currency trading market in the world, the forex market is open continuously during the work week. Most forex trading is done by experienced individuals, such as bankers.

Forex trading is typically conducted through a forex broker, but there is nothing to prevent anyone from trading currencies on their own. With the help of forex trading, buyers and sellers may purchase the currency they require for their operations, and sellers who have earned currency can trade what they have for a more practical currency.

The biggest banks in the world control the forex market, and according to a poll published in The Wall Street Journal Europe, the top ten forex dealers account for roughly 73% of trading volume.

The remaining half of forex trading is, however, largely speculative, with dealers building up investments that they eventually hope to sell for a profit. All forex trading transactions are based on currency pairings, even if a currency's value rises or falls in relation to a wide variety of other currencies.

Therefore, even though the Euro may be "strong" relative to a basket of currencies, traders will only be dealing with one currency pair and may only be concerned with the Euro/US Dollar (EUR/USD) ratio. Changes in the relative prices of currencies may occur gradually or be brought on by particular events, such as the toxic debt crisis, which is currently playing out as this chapter is being written.

Finding current information on forex is not always simple. Thankfully, this book has the most recent forex information accessible. The foreign exchange market, often known as the currency market or "forex," is a global decentralized over-the-counter financial market used for currency trading. Financial hubs serve as the anchors for trade among a variety of different sorts of buyers and sellers around the clock, excluding weekends. The exchange rates between various currencies are set by the foreign exchange market.

You will now have some basic knowledge about forex. Even if you don't know everything, you have still done something important by broadening your knowledge.

Forex Trading Overview

Millions of trades are done every day on the Forex market, a place to exchange currencies. The phrases "foreign" and "exchange" are the direct origins of the word "Forex." Contrary to other trading platforms like the stock market, forex does not entail the trade of any tangible or fictitious assets. Instead, buying, selling, and trading amongst the currencies of various economies around the world is how forex is conducted. Trades are executed 24 hours a day, five days a week, as the Forex market is truly a global trading system.

Forex is also not constrained by any regulatory body, making it the only genuine free-market economic trading system accessible at the moment. It is far harder to even attempt to manipulate or corner the currency market when exchange rates are not under the control of any one organization. The forex market is the biggest market in the entire world due to all of the benefits associated with the forex system and the global scope of participation. Every single day, anything between 1 trillion and 1.5 trillion equivalent United States dollars is transacted on the foreign exchange market.

Forex primarily relies on the idea of "free-floating" currencies, which are best defined as those that are not backed by particular assets like gold or silver. Prior to 1971, the international Bretton Woods accord prevented a market like forex from functioning. This agreement said that all participating economies would work to keep the value of their national currencies near the value of the US dollar, which was held to the value of gold. The Bretton Woods Accord was broken in 1971.

As a result of the United States' massive deficit during the Vietnam War, they started creating more paper money than they could cover with gold, which led to a comparatively high degree of inflation. By 1976, every significant currency had abandoned the Bretton Woods-established monetary system and transitioned to a free-floating one. Because of this free-floating arrangement, the value of any nation's currency might vary greatly depending on how well that nation's economy was doing at the time.

Because each currency varies on its own, it is possible to profit from changes in the value of the many currencies. For instance, 1 euro used to be equivalent to 0.86 US dollars. A short time later, 1 euro was equivalent to 1.08 US dollars. Those who purchased Euros at 86 cents and sold them for 1.08 US dollars were able to profit by 22 cents on each Euro, which could translate to hundreds of millions of dollars in earnings for those who had a strong investment in the currency.

Everything in the forex market is dependent on fluctuating currency exchange rates. Sadly, very few individuals are aware that the currency rates they regularly see on the news and read about in newspapers may be able to work in their favor even if they were to make a tiny investment.

The US dollar and the euro are two of the most extensively traded currencies in the forex market since they are two of the most well-known currencies used in the market. A few other currencies, in addition to the two "kings of currency," have a solid reputation for Forex trading. Established Forex traders frequently use the Australian dollar, the Japanese yen, the Canadian dollar, and the New Zealand dollar. It's crucial to keep in mind that on most Forex services, you won't see a currency's whole name written out.

Every currency has its own symbol, similar to how stock market corporations have their own symbols based on their corporate names. Some of the crucial monetary symbols to know include:

USD - United States Dollar

EUR - The Euro

CAD - The Canadian Dollar

AUD - The Australian Dollar

JPY - The Japanese Yen

NZD - The New Zealand Dollar

Although the symbols may seem confusing at first, you will eventually become accustomed to them. Keep in mind that each currency's symbol logically develops from its name, which is typically an abbreviation.

With a little practice, you'll be able to recognize the majority of currency codes without having to look them up.

Some of the wealthiest people in the world have a sizable portion of their financial portfolios in forex. The richest man in the world, Warren Buffet, has more than $20 billion invested in various currencies on the forex market. His revenue portfolio often has well over $100 million in earnings from forex trades in each quartile.

Another prominent name in currency trading is George Soros, who is said to have earned more than $1 billion from a single trading day in 1992. Despite the fact that these kinds of trades are extremely uncommon, he was nevertheless able to acquire over $7 billion from three decades of trading on the forex market.

The method of George Soros also demonstrates that you don't have to be overly risky to earn money on Forex; rather, his conservative approach entails taking significant profits out of the market, even when the trend of his numerous investments appears to be continuing to rise.

Fortunately, you don't need to invest millions of dollars to benefit from forex. Many people have reported success with initial contributions ranging anywhere from $10,000 to as little as $100. Due to the vast range of economic requirements it can accommodate, forex is a popular trading platform for all classes, from those firmly rooted in the lower rungs of the middle class to the world's richest individuals. The ability to access the forex market is a relatively new development for those at the lower end of the income spectrum. Many businesses have started delivering systems that are more user-friendly in recent years, enabling the lower initial investments and increased flexibility that are currently seen in the market.

Now, you can begin regardless of your financial situation. Although it is possible to jump straight in and begin investing, it is best to ensure that you have a better understanding of the ins and outs of Forex trading before you begin.

The Forex market is one that has the potential to be both lucrative and interesting, but in order to make it work for you, it's crucial that you understand how the system operates. Like other rewarding pursuits, mastering the Forex market requires a lot of practice. Numerous websites provide just this, the practice of simulating foreign exchange.

It is always a good idea to make sure you are familiar with all of the specifics of the website you are about to use because the services offered by online practice sites vary from site to site. For instance, a few online brokers will give you a practice account for a few weeks before terminating it and switching you to a live account, which means you might end up using your own money before you're ready to. Finding a website that provides an unlimited practice account is always a smart idea. Having a practice account enables you to learn how to trade with zero risk.

Even the most experienced Forex traders might benefit from continuing to use the practice account while using a live account. Utilizing a practice account with no risk allows you to test out novel trading approaches and venture into uncharted territory. If the technique is successful, you will be able to apply it to your real account. If the approach doesn't work, you know how to stop using it without losing any actual money.

Of course, using a no-risk account alone won't get you very far. You must invest your own money in Forex in order to profit from it. Since it would be absurd to fly to other nations to buy and sell other currencies, there are numerous websites that you may use to transact in virtual currency. You must conduct your research to determine which website you wish to open an account with because nearly all online brokerage systems have unique features to offer you.

To create your account, all brokers will need specific information about you. They will require information from you in order to communicate with you, such as your name, mailing address, phone number, and email address. They also ask for information such as your social security number, passport number, or tax identification number in order to identify who you are. They are obligated by law to have this information so they can stop fraudulent trade.

When you open an account, they may also gather a variety of personal data about you, such as your gender, birth date, occupation, and employment status.

Now that you have practiced forex trading and set up your live account, it is time to fully enter this lucrative yet dangerous industry. You do need to start out with money in order to make money with forex. It is possible to trade with very little capital, but doing so will also result in very tiny gains. Great payments will only come with high risks, as is the case with many other exchange systems. You can't expect to start making millions as soon as you invest money in the market, but if you don't invest at least a three-digit amount, you can't expect to make any money at all.

Do not invest your entire life savings in a single trade since, as the majority of Forex brokers would caution you, you could lose money in the foreign exchange market. Always use funds for trading that you could live without. This will make sure that even if you have a bad deal and lose a lot of money, you won't end up on the streets and will be able to bounce back later.

So how does trading currencies operate? Trading logically always occurs in pairs. For instance, a typical exchange would be the US dollar to the yen.

This is how USD/JPY is represented. It can be a little difficult to quote a trade, but with repetition, it becomes as easy as reading your mother tongue.
The base currency in a Forex quote is the first currency listed (in this case, USD in USD/JPY), and the base currency is always one in a quote. This means that the quote would be expressed as 1/2 if (again, hypothetically) one USD were equal to two JPY.

We use pips when trading forex. An acronym for "percentage in point" is "pip." A difference between a certain decimal place in a number and the same decimal place in a different number We track the gains and losses of a currency's value in relation to another's using pip values.

Let's look at an illustration.

Let's say a value is expressed as 1.0001/1.0004. Due to the three-number discrepancy at the fourth decimal place, this would indicate a 3-pip spread. Most currency pair conversions use the fourth decimal place. The USD/JPY currency pair is the only one that does not, and it rounds to the second decimal point. A USD/JPY quote with a 3-point spread, for instance, would seem as follows:

1.01/1.04.

Leverage is a very typical feature of the foreign exchange market. Trading on margin, also referred to as "leveraged trading," is a way to increase the amount of money you are making. Leverage trading involves borrowing a set amount of money from your broker and using that money to complete your deal. This enables you to trade with more money than you are actually spending, allowing you to earn more profits than you would normally be able to.

Risks are associated with using leverage in trading. If you use more money than you normally would, you risk losing more money if a trade doesn't go well. The risks are worthwhile, though, as a large margin of victory results in a hefty payment. As previously noted, it is definitely a good idea to experiment with leveraged trading on a practice account before using it extensively on a live account so you can get a sense of how it functions.

Now that you are knowledgeable about how forex trading operates, there are a few things about foreign exchange that you ought to be aware of. Forex is similar to the stock market in that it has many advantages and risks, but if you're going to put your time and money into this system, you should be fully informed of all the variables that could affect your choice to invest in the currency market.

Due to the various factors that may change the value of the currency over time, forex is generally a tough topic to express an opinion on. Supply and demand is a key problem for the forex industry because the world is always changing, with oil being one important product. The currency of all countries throughout the world is typically described as a large "melting pot" since all of the interchanging political disagreements, national conflicts, and possibly war conflicts mix together as a whole, changing the nature of forex every second!

Despite issues like supply and demand, as well as the general "melting pot" problem, there are many advantages to forex, one of which is the ability to profit from long-term stock. The share of electronic trading in the FX market (short for foreign exchange) increased by 7% from 2005 to 2008 due to the favorable elements of forex. Despite the contentious nature of the forex market, it is nevertheless widely acknowledged and favored by many countries around the world.

Most of the institutions that recognize forex engage in both monetary and fiscal policy. Both policies depend on how the country views its economy and the standards it has set. The country's economic situation has a significant impact on the government's budget deficits or surpluses against the country, which may seriously harm the national currency.

Another aspect of the country's deficit spending is what it already has in terms of necessities for its citizens and society. The budget for meeting other needs of the populace, such as those relating to technology, improvements in already existing items, etc., is greater the more the country already possesses prior to trade. Even if a country has plenty of essentials, greed can hurt the economy by making government officials demand "unnecessary" goods, hurting or "wasting" the country's finances in the process.

This downward trend might spell disaster for the nation and damage the currency's reputation as a force for good. There are some nations that produce more of a certain good (such as the oil mentioned above), with the Middle East dominating that sector of global trade;

Due to the Middle East's severe poverty, which is brought on by deficit spending and a lack of other resources, they need a higher oil price in order to preserve their current level of prosperity. Many nations engage in this tactic, known as "flights to quality," in an effort to survive in the global economic system that now exists. Global inflations, which vary greatly from place to place, drive leveraged financing and interest rates. As purchasing power declines due to inflation, the value of the currency also does.

In some circumstances, a nation may observe the trends it follows and take action in advance to prevent any mishaps that may have occurred in the past. Sometimes the nation will purchase or sell more of a product than necessary, a situation known as "overbuying" or "overselling." Due to a lack of consideration and bogus reasoning, this might either help or devastatingly harm the nation.

As stated in a letter from the chairman of Forex, "What began as a market for experts is now drawing traders from all over the world and of all skill levels."

Although it is impacted by interest rates and leveraged financing and can increase or decrease exchange rate risks, forex trading can be a terrific way for a nation to have a well-integrated economy and make rapid money. Forex can help in these industries by helping you invest in stocks that are most likely to be profitable for a long time and by helping you investigate these firms for further background information and references that you need to know. The inter-bank market, which is made up of the biggest investment bank firm in the Forex market with various levels of access, has "spreads" that are broken down into bid and ask prices. The term "better spread" refers to enormous numbers of transactions involving significant sums of money being traded and only asking for a little amount of difference, which is desired by many investors.

If users are aware and have a basic understanding of the subject, the Forex market is just as stable and safe as the stock market. Because of the incredibly inexpensive shares that replaced the shares that had originally cost hundreds of dollars, the 1929 stock market crash was caused by a lack of foresight. Leveraged finance was present at the time of the stock market crash and the New Deal proposal by Franklin D. Roosevelt. It was used to help stabilize the economy at the time.

Before the Great Depression, the United States was tremendously affluent and prosperous and had no idea what could happen as a result of irresponsible spending. This is the outcome of deficit spending, and it shows how it can harm a society in less than ten years! When investing in forex, keep in mind that there are challenges that must be overcome in order to be successful, along with both potential positive and negative consequences.

People who participate in the forex industry keep in mind the risks and benefits that may one day befall them as a result of numerous catastrophic events, such as the Great Depression that occurred in the United States. More effort and thought put out by an individual, group, or organization in the forex market will lead to more indications of prosperity.

In comparison to people like Warren Buffet and George Soros, they have succeeded via hard work, perseverance, and a variety of security-related programs and research. Forex is a vast subject that affects various people on a daily basis, ranging from some of the world's richest people to others who are only testing it to see what potential it has for them. Forex may not benefit everyone who invests in it, but if enough output is increased in efforts to improve the economy, it is most definitely something that everyone should experience first-hand.

Forex Trading Myths

Due in large part to the popularity of online stock trading, forex trading has grown in popularity over the past several years. However, its popularity also brings with it inescapable hype, myths, and occasionally outright lies. Even though many of these misconceptions are unfounded, they do cast doubt on the Forex market, and some of them may even cost novice currency traders money.

The following is a list of the most prevalent forex myths:

Trading currencies is simple.

First, the reality: Starting a forex trading business and buying and selling currencies online are both simple processes. But achieving success and earning money is far from simple. It necessitates training, time, and practice. Of course, there are gifted traders who pick up new skills quickly, but generally speaking, beginning traders should set aside some of their time for self-education, practice, and strategy development.

Forex is a game of chance.

This is a fallacy that applies to all types of trading, including stocks, bonds, futures, options, etc. Since it only deals with the performance, structure, and behavior of national or regional economies as a whole, as well as their interrelationships with one another, Forex is, in fact, the essence of macroeconomics in its purest form. This makes it even more unique than other types of market trading.

The world's best gamblers would be all the national economic administrators, advisors, consultants, and pupils if this were the case. Instead, we are all studying psychology, economics, technical analysis, and fundamental analysis.

Forex is a swindle.

High-yielding investment programs (HYIPs) started claiming to make money on the forex market, which caused forex to receive some negative press. More recently, two businesses—one in New York and the other an online trading platform—were shut down for defrauding investors of millions of dollars. Thankfully, prison sentences have been handed out for tarnishing the reputation of a respectable, well-controlled, and law-abiding sector. Forex is actually a legitimate currency market where everyone may trade and make their own judgments; therefore, it's hardly a fraud.

As a Forex trader, the only frauds you should be concerned about are brokers and marketers who promote Forex books, foolproof trading systems, guaranteed returns, and other "too good to be true" items. Only wealthy people can trade forex. It was accurate.

Forex is now accessible to everyone thanks to the quick development of high bandwidth in the typical Internet connection and the financial support of the biggest financial organizations on the planet. You only need $1 to get started in trading.

Forex trading is utterly arbitrary.

Although the quick changes in the forex market may appear impulsive and arbitrary, this is a total fiction. There must be a countertrade to your order when you place a trade. In no way is it arbitrary. Long-term changes in currency pairs are not at all random. Although there is a range of probability, it is not random and can be foreseen, managed, and influenced by global, regional, and national economies.

In forex, there is a "Holy Grail." Some people would rather think they can discover a plan that will generate millions of dollars and be effective forever. Sadly, there is no evidence to support such an assumption.

Successful traders constantly adjust their techniques to reflect the state of the market. The majority of the time, a successful Forex strategy cannot be described as a straightforward collection of principles; rather, it requires flexibility and constant adjustment.

Yes, in three years, a housewife from the Philippines who started a $25 forex trading account grew it to $2.6 million. She is an incredible dealer. She perfected her trading approach through study, practise, learning, and regular adjustment.

Brokers compete with their clients in trading. To put it briefly, this is both true and false. There must be a counter transaction being executed at the same moment as you execute a trade. If not, your broker counters it to cover your trade until they can find another trader to make a similar move in the other direction, thereby reducing their exposure. Keep in mind that forex brokers attempt to maintain as little market exposure as possible because they primarily rely on the spread, which is the difference between currency pairs, to generate revenue.

Forex trading is fraught with danger.

This is real and not a myth. There are no certainties in trading or investing, just as in any other activity, and you run the risk of losing every penny you put up. It is prevented by using effective risk management strategies, although it could still occur. Please make sure that the $25 you use to open an account is not the $25 you need to buy infant food. Additionally, although it is technically possible, I have never heard of someone losing more money than they initially invested (current internet trading mechanisms prevent it).

Getting Started with Forex Trading

When you trade currencies on the Forex market or in any other way, you are engaging in currency speculation, and that is all it is. This implies that, as with any business, there is some risk associated with trading foreign currencies, but you can and should take measures to reduce it. You can always establish a limit on the downside of any deal, which implies defining the maximum loss you're willing to take if the market moves against you.

Where to Start

The best way to prevent losing money in the forex market is to fully understand what you're doing. When there are parts you don't understand, find a reputable Forex trading forum and ask a ton of questions.

Many of the people who frequently respond to your questions on this will have excellent Forex trading blogs, and this will likely not only give you the answers to your questions but also provide you with ton of links to excellent websites. Be on the lookout for forex trading scams while remaining cautious. Be careful with your money and do your research thoroughly before you part with any of your hard-earned money.

All transactions in forex, which is all about foreign exchange, start with a currency pair, such as the euro and the dollar. The fundamental instrument for forex trading is the exchange rate, which is expressed as a ratio between the values of the two currencies, such as EUR/USD = 1.4086.

This amount, known as the "Forex rate," indicates that one euro would have been worth 1.4086 US dollars at that particular moment. This ratio is always expressed to four decimal places. It indicates that you might see a foreign exchange rate of EUR/USD = 1.4086 or 1.4087 but never EUR/USD = 1.40865. The ratio's rightmost digit is designated as a "pip." Therefore, a change of 2 pips from EUR/USD = 1.4086 to 1.4088 would be deemed a change.

One pip is always the last unit of a transaction.

An investor purchasing 1000 Euros using dollars would have to spend $1,408.60 at the current exchange rate of EUR/USD = 1.4086. The investor might sell their 1,000 Euros for $1,502.00 and keep the $93.40 as profits if the exchange rate changed to EUR/USD = 1.5020. If this doesn't seem like a significant number to you, you must consider the total in its wider context. The Forex rate does not just change in a consistent manner when a market is rising or falling; rather, it oscillates, allowing for many benefits to be taken throughout the day as the rate moves around a trend.

If you think the value of the EUR/USD will decline, you might trade in a different way by exchanging your Euros for dollars and then buying them back once the exchange rate has shifted in your favor.

The usual "lot" is 100,000 units of any currency, which is the lowest limit trading size for the majority of forex operations. But there are many businesses that offer the ability to buy in significantly smaller numbers than this, and some internet searching will quickly find these.

Many advertisements claim that you only need a few hundred bucks to get started. You'll commonly hear the phrase "actions trading forex," which simply refers to the little guy trading forex. These types of small-scale trading platforms are sometimes referred to as "Forex micro trading."

With online forex trading, you have direct access to the forex market and a plethora of businesses that exist solely to do business with you.

While it may be appropriate to exercise caution when considering any Forex trading technique that is marketed, there are a few reliable ones out there. Most of them either use Forex charts or detect Forex trading signals through the use of these that inform the trader when to buy or sell. These signals will be comprised of a specific change in a Forex rate or trend and will have been developed by a Forex trader who has researched long-term market trends in order to recognize legitimate signals when they occur.

Many of the systems will employ Forex trading software that recognizes such signals from data inputs that are automatically acquired from sources of market data. Few traders use automated Forex trading software, which may initiate trades automatically when instructed to do so by signals.

If these seem too good to be true to you, search for online Forex trading systems that will let you try out a few dummy trades. By doing this, you may receive some Forex trading training by giving them a try before putting actual money on the line.

Be cautious, invest the time necessary to obtain excellent Forex trading instruction (again, this may be offered online), and set up your practice account to trade before attempting to go live. There is no reason why you shouldn't be successful at forex trading if you take care and take your time, so be persistent and patient!

Various Forex Trading Techniques

Currently, the hottest chance for earning money is through forex trading. Especially following the stock market meltdown, which left many people with scorched fingers. Now, if you've never traded foreign exchange, you might be asking how to get started. In this article, I discuss the four different forex trading methods, along with their advantages and disadvantages.

Let's begin, then:

Forex Signals

You can sign up for a forex signal service if you are new to forex trading and don't have a lot of time to learn how to trade the currency market. Today, there are numerous forex signal providers. You receive forex signals by email and SMS. You don't have to constantly monitor the market with these forex alerts. Just input "purchase" or "sell" as the service suggests. Finding a reliable forex signal service is the trick.

How do I do that?

Test the forex signals first on your practice account. Only by using a signal service's demo account can you determine how accurate the signals are. A new development has just begun. Professional forex traders that use their own funds to trade their own accounts have begun offering signal services.

You receive genuine live trading signals as these professional forex traders conduct their own trades on a live account. You also get $1,000 if that professional forex trader wins $1,000, and you lose $1,000 if they lose. With a trade copy tool that joins two or more MT4 accounts, you can copy their exact live trades. You don't need to worry too much about the signal quality because the professional trader is dealing with his or her own real money. Naturally, a professional forex trader will use extreme caution when trading with real money.

Second, the Trade Copier will automatically enter your buy or sell signals for you; you don't need to open your MT4 account all the time. Of course, you need to locate a successful professional trader who is willing to share their live trading account with you using a trade copy.

Forex Trade Robot

You can also use Forex Robot to automate your trading. Some effective forex robots have recently entered the market. Some traders have made a fortune with forex trading robots. The issue is that the majority of them were the people who created those robots.

You see, the fundamental issue with these robots is that they must constantly be tuned to account for shifting market conditions. Most new traders are unable to do this successfully since they don't know very much about forex trading. In addition to that, you also need to know a little bit of programming in order to succeed with a forex robot. Most new traders find it challenging. Forex robots are effective, but in order to use them, you must learn both forex trading and MQL4 programming. something that many new traders find challenging.

Most of the time, the merchants will make it seem as though a forex robot is the simplest way to trade forex. It only requires installation on your MT4 platform before it begins to generate income for you. Nothing is more false than the truth. Market conditions are always shifting. A working robot could begin to lose money as soon as market conditions shift.

Forex-managed accounts

Forex Managed accounts are operated by experienced forex traders who will trade your money according to your instructions in exchange for a fee of between 5 and 20%. You have the right to withdraw your funds at any time. You actually maintain full control over your finances. For those who didn't have the time to trade forex, managed forex accounts have been the go-to option.

Manual Forex Trading

You can trade forex on your own, yes. But in order to do it, you must master forex trading. This could take a while.

You'll also need to put your trading talents through a lot of practice. Learning forex trading is worthwhile, though. It is unquestionably the long-term solution and ought to be your ultimate objective.

Tools for Forex Trading

A trader has access to several Forex trading tools. Despite the abundance of such instruments, there are still a relatively small number of traders that achieve consistent gains. Therefore, the obvious question is: If forex trading tools don't make a successful trader, then what does?

Some of the tools needed to trade FX currencies are straightforward and simple. At the same time, there are just a select few others who aren't. However, these less obvious instruments still play a significant role in your performance in forex trading, even though they don't directly affect your trading outcomes.

One of the reasons why it is so tough for forex traders to succeed is that they are unable to see how everything interacts with one another in the currency markets. The ability to see the bigger picture is essential for becoming a successful trader since it affects how you use your trading instruments to extract gains from the markets.

Beginner traders and experienced traders differ in that:

Most new traders just consider the bare minimum necessary to get started, whereas experienced, seasoned traders frequently work to make the best use of the resources at their disposal.

Retail traders typically have the least information and the least influence over how foreign exchange rates are set in the game of forex trading. On the other hand, even though banks and other large financial institutions have access to sophisticated forex trading tools, this does not mean that you, as a retail trader, need all of these tools to succeed in forex trading. However, in order to succeed in forex trading, you must have all of the necessary trading tools.

So, what do you need to get started in forex trading?

The Essential Forex Trading Tools to Get Started

These are the fundamental instruments for forex trading that you obviously need in order to trade foreign currencies, but they are not the only ones needed for successful forex trading:

Your forex trading account

Your forex trading platform

Your currency trading strategy

Your Forex Trading Capital Risk

Most often, inexperienced forex traders tend to believe that this is all they need to do to become extremely profitable in the forex markets. Do you see how easy and straightforward it is?

It is true that this is all you need to get started trading. What is less obvious is that while this is what you need to begin trading, it's not necessarily what is required to do so profitably.

Being successful at forex trading requires you to travel a path of learning and development as a trader. From point A to point B—consistent forex trading profits—it is a journey.

To believe that a newbie trader can achieve phenomenal success using only these four trading instruments is equivalent to believing that a soaring 100-story building can be built with only a pencil, a piece of paper, and four bricks. Other components and tools are used to create your forex trading business, but because they are in the background of what is happening, it is easy to overlook or minimize their significance.

We would have a lot more traders who are successful and wealthy if these four tools were all that were necessary for successful trading, wouldn't we?

Improving your ability to use the fundamental forex trading tools

To succeed as a forex trader, you must improve your abilities. The product's quality is a result of the craftsman's skill. The more highly trained you are, the better able you will be to comprehend and use the subtleties of forex trading instruments.

On the surface, it could seem that technical expertise would be needed to use these forex trading instruments. Understanding how your trading platform functions, how technical indicators are created, what they signify, and how to best combine them to create a forex trading system.

Success in forex trading is not a two-dimensional phenomenon that only involves your trading account and a trading strategy. In truth, it's a multifaceted concept that embraces you as a whole person and not just as a trader. You must learn a forex trading method that is appropriate for you, the best risk and money management techniques, how to build a daily forex trading routine that aligns with your actual life goals, how to maintain your records, and other supporting skills.

And these abilities as a trader cannot be purchased with money. To build your trading talents, it takes patience, perseverance, and discipline. Not only that, but it also takes actual trading experience to comprehend your emotions and know how to control them in your forex trading business.

Although it may seem like a lot of work and study is required to become a successful forex trader, it is definitely possible. Just keep in mind that it won't happen over night; if it does, you'll be really let down. Even the best traders are always picking up new knowledge about the markets, the nuances of trading, and themselves as people and traders.

Even if you can shorten the learning process with the correct forex trading education and mentorship, you'll typically still need to go through the experience of discovering what it takes to be a successful forex trader.

Forex Trading Timing

For effective and efficient Forex trading, it is essential to understand when the best times are to trade. The Forex market is open 24 hours a day during the trading week, but just because it is open around the clock doesn't mean prices are always changing in a way that makes a certain market worthwhile to trade. The forex market makes money when it is dynamic and active, not when it is still and relatively quiet.

Therefore, as a Forex trader, you must be aware of the times that are the most active for trading, as this will greatly aid you in the timing of both your entries and exits as you traverse the markets. The two most active Forex trading sessions are the London and New York sessions, when price activity offers the best trading conditions. The Asian trading session is frequently less volatile and hence less likely to cause significant changes in the several Forex pairs.

The forex market has three unique trading sessions that begin in Australia and Asia, travel across the world to Europe, and culminate in North America. Every day, trade in New York comes to an end. The following are the various Forex trading hours:

- The Asian trading session, which includes Australia and New Zealand, begins at 6:00 p.m. Eastern Time and ends at 4:00 a.m.

- The London trading session begins at 3 a.m. Eastern Time and ends at 12 p.m. Eastern Time.

- New York trading session: it starts at 8:00 a.m. Eastern Time and ends at 5:00 p.m. Eastern Time.

As you can see from the list of appropriate times to trade forex above, there are times during each day when the sessions overlap.

These are the times of day when volume and volatility often reach their highest levels. The best time to trade forex is often thought to be when the London and New York trading periods overlap between 8 a.m. and 12 p.m. EST. The reason this is regarded as the best time to trade is that it occurs when the world's two busiest trading centers intersect; as London trading closes, New York trading begins, and they are both open at the same time for four hours each trading day. Because of this, many traders only trade within this 4-hour window because it typically offers the best liquidity and volatility.

Knowing which currency pairings to trade in addition to the best times to engage in Forex trading is helpful. In general, the "major" forex currency pairs are the finest; they are regarded as the best forex pairs to trade primarily because they have the lowest spreads and greatest liquidity. This means that the major currency pairings have lower transaction costs and move more predictably than "exotic" currency pairs, which have a tendency to leap around and behave in an illogical manner. The final step in studying Forex is to ensure that you are aware of the best times to trade and the best Forex pairs to use.

Regarding the Systems

You can find a ton of websites online that provide guidance on the most innovative and effective trading strategies you may use in the Forex market.
New traders are frequently duped into purchasing these trading techniques in the hope of making more money. Avoid making the same mistake. Before deciding to use these trading techniques, you must first evaluate them.

Scammers abound on the internet, and some trading systems are either fake or unreliable. You must choose only the best and most dependable systems.
If you use reliable trading methods regularly and with discipline, they may help you make a lot of money.

The Spirit of Us

Many Forex traders are looking for the best trading methods that are available online, and it's possible that you're doing the same. You must be practical when looking for an effective method, so you must take several things into account. Few systems are actually challenging to comprehend.

Make sure you understand the system's rationale before purchasing it. You can only efficiently use the system to your advantage by comprehending its logic. You can assess whether the trading system is overall reasonable and straightforward from your own point of view by carefully reviewing it. You can go a long way if you believe you can stick with the trading system and are confident in its reasonable core logic.

In the forex market, having a smart trading strategy is essential. You need to put in more work on your research and run a few trials. How can you tell if a system is good? A fantastic method is one that can be used in the long run and has a steady stream of income.

To begin with, it is essential that you have a backup strategy in place in case of a downturn. You are able to maintain your position despite the financial setbacks by doing this. You must be emotionally prepared, and once you have a large sum of money, you must be wise about how you use or spend it.

When using a specific trading technique in the Forex market, you shouldn't anticipate seeing returns right away. It's true that you can make a lot of money trading forex, but you also run the risk of losing your initial investment. You must be extremely cautious and patient when making trading judgments. Give the system enough time to function; for example, a few months to a year may be sufficient to evaluate whether the system is lucrative or not. You must make sure that trade transactions during this time are rational and consistent.

The majority of trading systems available today deliver Forex data in almost real time, but a select few only offer simulations of the underlying logic based on previous data. You can still use the system to your advantage if you believe that the fundamental reasoning is clear and sound.

The foreign exchange market is rapidly altering or changing. Your trading system should be able to quickly adapt to these changes and adjustments. Better performance is not always guaranteed by complicated systems; instead, it is preferable to select a system that is simple to use and intuitive.

You may already have a superb trading technique that will work for you if you research the important trends in the forex market. Choose a system that is disciplined and logical. Avoid using your emotions when performing the trade because it could be the beginning of your undoing.

You can find a variety of applications for trading forex. Every piece of trading software on the market has its own perks and downsides. You must be aware of your needs in order to choose the best software for Forex trading. What systems are available to you, then?

Most of the market-available software aids in reducing the stress of trading in the forex market. The forex market is open for longer hours than the stock market; in fact, it is open around the clock.You can keep track of everything happening in the forex market with the use of effective software. You cannot possibly spend your entire day staring at the computer looking for market updates.

You can go about your normal daily activities while using the software. When you have the time to research and analyze the stock market, you may simply use the trading software to keep track of the day's events.

The difficult chores will all be handled by the software for you. The trading software may automatically monitor all Forex market activity around the clock. The degree of the software's independence may be chosen by the trader. Most traders, especially if they are also extremely busy with their work, leave all the dirty work to the program.

Here is a really good illustration of how trading software functions:

You made the decision to invest in a specific trade. Because of a few negative changes in the market, you started losing money while you were doing the laundry or maybe even in the grocery store. If your software is effective, it will automatically exit trades once it detects a change that could be considered unfavorable in the Forex market.

Some trading platforms place a strong focus on signal indications, generators, and other market patterns. You could gain a lot from this software because it will allow you to confidently trade without having any doubts. You see, this kind of program employs tried-and-true, sophisticated mathematical techniques. Through the use of this kind of software, forex moguls are making significant profits. The program has been tried and tested. In reality, this kind of software can assist you in choosing a trading strategy with accuracy thanks to its sophisticated algorithms and trend indicators. The indicators may provide you with precise forex data as well as trading advice.

Software packages for combinations are also available. You can use these whether you're a newbie or an experienced trader. This kind of software can provide useful trend indicators or signal generators while also keeping track of changes in the Forex market.

What type of software you purchase and use doesn't really matter. You can use the software for however long you like, as long as it functions for you. For traders who are hesitant to purchase a specific piece of software, test versions are also available.

Choose the appropriate software program with care if you intend to engage in forex trading. Trading in a really complicated market isn't as simple as you might believe, and you need to be ready for everything with the aid of trading software.

Market Expectations and Forex Volatility

Volatility, or the propensity for change that may have an impact on your earnings in the stock market, is common in domestic markets but is far more pronounced and much stronger in the foreign exchange market. What elements influence the value of money on the Forex market, and is there any way to manage this?

Devaluation and Revaluation

Devaluation is the intentional decrease of a currency's value in comparison to other currencies as assessed by a government agency. The U.S. dollar is now only worth nine units of the foreign currency, for instance, if it was once worth ten units before it was devalued by ten percent. This lowers the exchange rate, increasing the price of any foreign-currency purchases for people dealing in U.S. dollars. Additionally, trading goods in US dollars makes them less expensive in the foreign country. Inverse value changes are also possible, increasing the value of the foreign currency. This was a reference to revaluation.

While it may appear that manipulating a country's currency value on purpose is "cheating" or giving oneself an unfair advantage because it lowers the price of imported goods and raises the value of exports, there are restrictions in place to prevent this. The International Monetary Fund's (IMF) charter helps to forbid such actions and enforce the policy.

There are strategies you can use to benefit from devaluation and revaluation, which will be covered in more detail later. What occurs, though, when the value of a foreign currency changes as a result of market fluctuations rather than deliberate decreases or increases by the federal government or a federal bank? What impact do price growth and decline have on the stock market?

Appreciation and Depreciation

Depreciation and the lifespan of a car are simply comparable. As soon as you drive a new car off the lot, its value is almost halved. This represents a drastic decline. The car's value will decline over the following few years, however, at a more moderate rate. This is also seen as depreciation.

Currency appreciation and depreciation are changes in the currency's value that are motivated more by market forces than by governmental decree. For instance, in 1998, the Central Bank of Russia announced the coming depreciation of the ruble in an effort to repay certain loans. Over time, the current currency rate of six rubles to one dollar would decrease to 9.5 rubles to one dollar, or a depreciation of 34%.

However, before the transformation, there was a generalized panic in the formerly Communist country, and the value of the ruble fell as a result of many Russians choosing to sell their securities before they reached maturity. Following the revelation, the Russian ruble lost an astounding 25% of its value in a single day.

When the U.S. stock market crashed in the 1920s, a similar catastrophe happened. At that point, there was a widespread panic, and individuals flocked to the banks to withdraw cash that wasn't available or to trade in securities and unmatured stock options. People actually contributed to the crash by running to the bank rather than avoiding it.

On the other hand, a country is more likely to experience inflation or a rise in the retail value of goods sold to the general population if its currency appreciates too quickly.

While inflation is unavoidable, it can at least be moderated by using currency valuation. A vehicle can also be associated with appreciation. Men frequently buy old cars and enjoy restoring them to their former splendor. By doing this, they significantly raise the vehicle's value or appreciate it.

There is an inherent market risk, or the possibility of daily loss due to price fluctuations in securities caused by fluctuating exchange rates and market volatility.

There is no way to spread this type of risk because it will always have an impact on investments to a certain extent. Certain investment types or methods, on the other hand, that are safer or more secure, can help balance some risk.

In later chapters, we'll examine long and short positions, short selling, stop orders, and other strategies for preventing a significant loss on your investments. These choices consist of the capability to predetermine your purchase or sale price for a certain commodity as well as the use of numerous predetermined order levels to place orders and complete transactions.

Of course, don't fool yourself into thinking that you can exclude all potential risk elements from the market. There is always a cloud hanging over your head that is just waiting to burst; all it takes is a tiny pinprick. Even though the idea of playing the stock market implies risk and excitement by definition, you should always use prudence. The following chapter will help you gain a better understanding of reality and what it entails to balance your risk factor with a sense of reality, or your ego with your id.

Forex Scams

Forex (foreign currency exchange) is a somewhat uncontrolled market with significant potential for both gains and losses. High potential for profit and lax regulation are the two variables that have drawn con artists from all over the world. These con artists use the allure of forex to defraud naive investors out of millions of dollars. Let me begin by demonstrating an example of a current forex scam.

I can easily uncover a few forex frauds on Google in just a few minutes. Take this one as an example:

The business purchased Google advertising space, so the first page of my search returns the company's website. The webpage says "Minimum Deposit: $5000, Maximum Deposit: $999,999, Investment Length: 30 Days, Guaranteed 200% Interest Per Month, Quick Withdrawals!

For a new trader in forex, it sounds fantastic. I just need to transfer them my money, and I'll start earning 200% per month. Wow!

If you keep reading, you'll discover that they use a lot of flowery language to describe their trading practices. They discuss the "security" of the money and the "stability" of their business. They have headings like "professionalism," "reliability," "trust," and my personal favorite, "process ability," on the "about us" page.

Under "Process Ability," they write, "Correct forecast of reversal of exchange rates outflow by using timely analysis of our department's received news, processing, and position control during technical and fundamental analysis." Within five seconds of reading, a REAL Forex trader can detect the hoax on this website. To the uninformed, who has heard of the enormous potential in forex, this may appear to be a dream come true.

So how does a novice Forex trader locate genuine Forex products and avoid Forex scams?

1. To start, keep in mind the proverb, "If it seems too good to be true, it probably is." In the world of forex, there isn't even such a thing as guaranteed returns, let alone a monthly return of 200%. Forex trading can be quite rewarding, but it is difficult and hardly ever consistent on a weekly basis. Beware if you see a forex company making such claims, especially one that uses automated forex systems.

2. Investigate the business offering the opportunity. In the situation we just outlined, it only takes a brief glance at the company's website registration to discover that the story is inconsistent. The company claims to have started in June, despite the fact that the website was registered in July of this year. They also provide bogus business contact details during site registration.

3. Never relinquish control of your finances. You should never have to transmit your money to a forex broker who is not fully regulated. You still have

control over your finances and your Forex account if you choose to have someone manage your money for you.

4. Interact with the individuals behind the Forex **opportunity**. Many Forex trades are completely legal. If a business opportunity is genuine, they will be more than happy to speak with you personally. Never invest in any forex product without getting in touch with the people in charge of it.

5. Does the business communicate the risks associated with trading foreign exchange? A dangerous investment is forex. A corporation is deceiving you if it won't accept that. Whether you are thinking of a managed Forex account, an automated Forex trading system, Forex training, Forex trade signals, or any other Forex product, it makes no difference. The hazards of trading forex must be made clear to you if they are offering you anything related to it.

6. Refrain from letting emotion control you. There is something intriguing about the potential to make 200% every month with a guarantee. This excitement frequently makes people oblivious to reality. They want to believe something is true so badly that they fail to see the obvious.

A viable investing possibility is forex. Every day, thousands of forex traders earn a sizable living by trading the forex market. Don't let yourself fall for any Forex scams that seem too good to be true, though. Because they are. Use common sense and

the advice I've given above to prevent becoming the
next Forex scam victim.

Automated Forex Trading

Are you a person of discipline? According to seasoned Forex traders, the only people who are successful in the market are those that maintain their discipline, whether they succeed or fail. The way traders conduct their trades has changed as a result of automated forex trading. If you're an experienced Forex trader, using these automatic systems will undoubtedly be beneficial for you.

Be warned that the majority of trading techniques marketed or offered online are viewed as rubbish and worthless for newcomers to the Forex market. These systems frequently provide tested simulations and highly promoted ineffective marketing techniques. By using "junk" trading strategies, you run the risk of losing your money.

Automation

There are simple trading strategies available online that, when used correctly and regularly, may result in larger returns. You see, intricate methods don't always guarantee success, so be very careful while choosing the best Forex system. The ease of operation of an automated trading system increases with its simplicity.

For example, if you believe that a certain currency will sustain a four-week high, buy it. You can sell low-standing currency before the price drops even further if you have it.

This strategy, which is also known as a breakout, bases all of your trades on the highs and lows of the Forex market. You'll soon be able to access the major industry trends.

Large trends frequently last for several weeks, months, or even years. The entire system runs automatically, and the rules are very objective. One system, referred to as a Forex robot, may run for fifteen minutes each day. This forex robot was created by trader Richard Donchian.

If you're looking for a simple system, the Forex robot might be right for you. Traders that favor complex trading systems frequently have higher expectations for this system and would want to choose a different system that can live up to those expectations. The Forex robot is easy to use and can assist you in determining the top and bottom options.

Spending enough time and effort allows successful Forex traders to make well-informed trading selections. As a wise trader, you shouldn't move too quickly. Allow the system to function. Don't believe the fallacy that more expensive, sophisticated systems are more effective. If you take Forex trading seriously, you can make a lot of money with little effort.

Keep an eye on current market trends. You are able to use the Forex robot since it is rational, very easy to use, and consistently works if you believe it will work for you in light of the current trends in the forex market.

You can see how the automated trading system works by downloading it for free from the internet. Check the Forex robot's history if you think it is just more rubbish like all the other programs. Try to look at reviews and ratings to learn more about this wonderful and effective solution.

Today's world is vastly different from that of long ago. Many of the simple jobs of today are now completed mechanically. You are able to use the Forex robot if you want an automated Forex system. Hurry and look for this method online; if you'd like, you can also check out Richard Donchian's website to learn more about it. You will gain a lot from this system in the long term. Don't put too much effort into learning about the Forex market because you can get a lot done with the help of an automatic method.

Few people really struggle with forex trading. The reason for this is that they didn't devote enough time to researching market patterns and thorough technical analysis, which is why they made this mistake. Forex charts are quite important, and you need to understand how they are created. As you likely already know, if you want to make significant gains, you must keep up with the fast-paced atmosphere of the forex market. Both market indicators and technical analysis may definitely be of assistance to you.

Indicators are really useful, especially when you're about to transact in the forex market. These indicators typically give you information about the likelihood of market behavior, but they are unable to accurately predict the certainty of currency values.

Technical indicators are very crucial when trading foreign exchange. To identify market patterns, you can mix the indicators to make your very own trading strategy. As a successful trader, you must be able to recognize current or major trends, short-term trends, and intermediate-term trends. If you can do this, you'll be able to hold a strong position in the forex market, where you may make significant gains.

Given how frequently the Forex market changes, you must establish a standard for using technical indicators. You must be able to integrate the necessary indications if you want to make forecasts with the maximum likelihood and accuracy. You are able to ascertain the price trends of the currencies you would like to trade by doing this.

Even if your judgment is sound, you still need to take other things into account in order to maximize your returns from your transactions. Take your profits and halt trading temporarily if you're having a bad day on the forex market.

This is a wise decision since if you stay longer (hoping to get your money back), you risk losing more of your initial investment. There is no need to prepare for a significant change when currency values are fluctuating within a so-called tight range and aren't going in any particular direction. Find a different currency to trade that has higher profit margins.

With so many technical indicators available, you can find combinations that are most effective for you.

Never give up if you ever have some setbacks in forex trading, because that is normal. When using technical indicators, you must allow enough time for your own research and analysis.

There are too many factors to consider finishing it in a few short minutes. However, be sure to move quickly when making your trading decisions. Because the Forex market won't slow down just for you. The only person who needs to adapt to the fast-paced atmosphere is you. Keep in mind that there are many traders out there who want to make money. You must maintain an edge over the opposition.

Technical analysis is not very easy to do, so you will need all the assistance you can obtain. If you want to learn more about this type of trading, you can speak with a broker or use some online Forex trading tools. The internet is widely accessible, and you can take advantage of it. Learn about these many technical indicators so that you may use them to determine market trends. You must become familiar with these technical indicators if you want to trade forex successfully.

Technical Indicators

The Forex market is said to be one of the most well-known locations among business professionals. Trading has existed in some form or another since the beginning of time. It goes without saying that this is a chance that offers better returns than the original investment.

As a result, it's a task that necessitates a thorough understanding of the various technical indicators that essentially prove to be quite useful. Combining two or more of them increases the likelihood that you will fully understand the actions you must take in order to continue with the possibility of making a big profit.

Things to watch

The use of technical indicators is advised for many traders. The professionals continue to believe in them. How much more can you provide a beginner like you? They are the mathematical equations that control the relevant indicators. Studies show that they are actually quite accurate, but that they don't really provide a thorough examination. These tools could show you market trends.

Your continued participation in the stock market indicates that you have a clear objective, which is to increase revenue and make a sizable profit. However, you must remember that the market is erratic. Meaning that because of its instability, a variety of changes could occur at any time. These indicators are the ideal instruments to use in determining if it is a suitable time to buy or sell commodities or securities.

It is also very important how you choose to use the indications. Always keep in mind that many formulas call for writing down the derivatives. This proves that the data isn't always straightforward. This is why it can be useful to consult multiple indicators to be able to create a clearer picture. After all, it will never hurt to double-check your conclusion's accuracy.

Fundamental Categories of Technical Indicators

Whether you want to trade stocks, commodities, or Forex, it pays to think about building a strong foundation that can act as your guide. Again, it's crucial to select those that you are confident have already been demonstrated to function and that you can use easily.

The Trendspotter Indicators

Just a few of the indicators that make up this group are moving averages, parabolic SAR, and MACD. You can determine the level at which you can start trading by paying attention to how the trends are moving.

The momentum marker Indicators

These are regarded as the oscillating indicators and

are the most precise in identifying overbought and oversold conditions. They also display the signals for any new trends. Just a few of the momentum trend indicators are stochastics, RSI, and CCI.

The indicators of volume

The name alone indicates that the price fluctuation is highly dependent on transaction volume. A price movement that is driven by high volume typically gathers a stronger signal than one that is driven by low volume. The force index, money flow index, ease of movement, Chaikin money flow, and several more are examples of these.

The Volatility Indicators

They frequently focus on the ranges that characterize the volume that underlies price behavior and fluctuation. The average true range, Bollinger bands, and envelopes are some typical examples.

Here are the four categories of technical indicators that will guide you as you attempt to achieve the best possible profits from the forex market.

Examining the Charts

Simple line graphs, bar graphs, or even candlestick graphs can be used to represent price data. These graphs display prices across specific time periods. These time spans could be anything between minutes and years, or any time period in between.

The simplest-to-understand line charts will provide you with a general picture of price movement. They don't provide the fine information of a bar or candlestick chart, but they do make it incredibly easy to see patterns and trends because they only display the closing price for the specified interval.

The length of a line on a bar chart indicates the price spread for that period of time. The greater the bar, the greater the price disparity between the interval's high and low prices.

Because the left tab displays the opening price and the right tab the closing price, it is simple to determine if the price increased or decreased at a glance. The bar will then show you the price variation. When printed, bar charts can be challenging to read, but most software charts have a zoom feature that makes it possible to read even closely spaced bars with ease.

Take a close look.

Candlestick charts, which were developed in Japan to

break down candlestick contracts, are extremely useful for evaluating FOREX prices. Candlestick charts and bar charts are quite similar in that they both display the high, low, open, and close prices for the given period of time. However, the color-coding makes candlestick charts much easier to read; typically, a green candlestick indicates a rising price and a red candlestick indicates a decreasing price.

The actual candlestick shape in relation to the other candlesticks nearby can tell you a lot about the price movement and substantially assist your analysis. The candlesticks will produce a variety of designs depending on the price spread. Many of the forms have somewhat strange names, but if you figure out the patterns, they're easy to identify and analyze.

Price charts are not frequently used by themselves; therefore, you must combine them with some technical indicators to get the full effect. Technical indicators are frequently divided into a few fairly broad categories. Indicators used to monitor and track market activity include trend indicators, strength indicators, volatility indicators, and cycle indicators, to name a few of the more popular ones.

Here is a list of some of the more popular indicators, along with a brief explanation.

Average Directional Movement Index (ADX):

The Average Directional Movement Index (ADX) can be used to determine whether the market is trending in one direction or the other, as well as how strong the trend is. It is thought that a trend is stronger if it has readings above twenty-five.

Moving Average Convergence/Divergence (MACD):

This illustrates the relationship between the moving averages, allowing you to assess the market's momentum. Any time the MACD crosses the signal line, the market is regarded as strong.

The stochastic oscillator:

The stochastic oscillator measures the market's strength or weakness by comparing the closing price to the price range over a given time frame. A currency is said to be overbought if its stochastic reading exceeds eighty. However, if the stochastic is below 20, the currency is regarded as being undersold.

The Relative Strength Indicator (RSI):

The Relative Strength Indicator (RSI) uses a scale of 1 to 100 to compare historical highs and lows. The RSI is deemed overbought if it rises above seventy and oversold if it falls below thirty.

Moving Average:

This is created by comparing the average price over a given time period to the average price over a different time period.

Simple Steps for Trading Forex

The most popular approach for aspiring traders these days is to explore the internet for information to apply right away to their live Forex trading account if they are interested in learning how to trade Forex successfully. The problem is that their search frequently takes them to places with lots of empty promises, bad ideas, pessimism, and a fixation on signs.

Many of the e-books currently for sale are full of incomplete or recycled concepts that the writers themselves don't use. Many authors make money by distributing these e-books to new Forex traders; they do not make money from forex trading.

The same people they have marketed this idea to are then financially supported by this easy access to Forex gurus, who feed the notion that forex trading is the key to the gravy train. Finally, much of what these Forex experts promote is a blatant misrepresentation of what it takes to trade forex for a living.

Guidelines

Trading in forex is not easy. You can succeed as a forex trader if you put in the necessary effort and approach it like any other talent. The reality is that it requires hard work and must be approached with the same level of dedication as any other profession.

The result of all these experts is that many Forex traders start out overly optimistic and with unattainable expectations. While having an optimistic outlook is admirable, it must be based on solid principles and realistic expectations.

New Forex traders frequently start their careers by purchasing a secret set of indicators, but they are swiftly penalised for their ignorance. The majority of these Forex traders then purchase yet another set of covert indicators until they lose interest and cease trading.

In actuality, many successful Forex traders went through this learning process. **This is only a concern if you are unwilling to grow from your errors.** To succeed, you must end this cycle of reliance on unreliable signs and guru methods.

By learning to think for yourself and realizing that, while anyone can trade forex, in order to be successful, you must become a forex trader, you first help yourself. Forex trading is easy; all you need is a trading account with funds in it, after which you can enter the foreign exchange market and start trading.

Being a forex trader requires more effort. You must advance from your initial level of having very little information to the point where you have a trading strategy, understand the principles and behavior of the forex market, are able to trade calmly, and understand that wins and losses are all part of being a trader.

1. Recognize Your Position in the Forex Market.

It's really important for you to realize that you are a very small fish in a very large sea. The majority of the liquidity in the forex market comes from powerful banks and knowledgeable institutional traders. These are the large fish. The enormous fish will gladly enjoy you as a small nibble. If you think it will be easy to take money from these large Forex traders, you're only deceiving yourself.

You must develop the ability to swim alongside these large fish and collect the same flows that they do. Swimming against them merely brands you as prey, and you will eventually be eaten.

2. Get Familiar with Studying Forex Charts.

Many new Forex traders mistakenly think that these large Forex traders have access to some kind of sophisticated trading strategy or use a hidden set of indicators, but this is simply not the case.

These prominent forex players are using straightforward but effective technical analysis methods, most frequently horizontal support and resistance, trading range identification, and fundamental themes.

The first step is to accept that the other key players in the market are very experienced and that their success is based on their knowledge of fundamental skills rather than the possession of any special indicators.

3. Cash Management.

It's crucial that you understand that as a beginner Forex trader, the focus is not on how much money you may make from Forex trading but rather on how you handle what you already have.

The most typical mistake made by all new traders is this. Beginner traders sometimes risk the majority of their money on one or two positions.

Professional traders don't deal this way because it isn't a viable way to conduct business. Everybody will have a streak of bad trades at some point in their career. Ten consecutive lost transactions is an average quantity. The question is, do you have a cash management strategy in place that will allow you to survive this?

4. Focus on the market.

Many new Forex traders open their charting software, activate the newest popular indicator or tool, and then proceed to place their trades in accordance with the tools' recommendations. This style of forex trading is unlikely to be very successful over the long term.

When these indications fail to produce the required gains, these traders quickly switch to a new set of indicators.

To choose the Forex trades that have the best possibility of success, you must focus on the Forex market and understand what the indicators are telling you.

Forex traders who are successful use indicators and tools. These tools don't make a successful trader on their own. According to research, many successful and unsuccessful traders use the same indications.

The key is that effective traders comprehend how the market behaves around the indicators and are aware of the true meaning of the signals.

The best way to do this is to switch between tools, choose those that support your trading strategy, understand how they operate, and then spend time in the market going over them.

5. Create your Transaction and Execute your Plan.

This is a general statement that seems to be misapplied to novice traders. Every trader should aim to gain pips on each Forex transaction in accordance with their trading strategy. Forex traders must approach each trade like a business decision by estimating their risk and carefully selecting their entry and exit locations. Those who don't expose themselves to significant losses when a trade fails.

Many new traders appear to lack the discipline to follow a plan for each trade.
So what typically happens is that a novice trader will see a potential set-up, choose some arbitrary amount to buy or sell with a quick estimate, and then place the trade without considering any risk or having an exit strategy.

Naturally, this method of trading may be successful in the short term, more as a result of luck than competence. But sooner or later, the trader's luck runs out and they are busted for kidnapping, which usually leads to a destroyed account.

Beginner traders often ask themselves at the outset, "How much will I make on this Forex trade?"

What is my probability of loss or risk? Is the first thing seasoned traders tend to ask themselves.

6. Your Brain is Both Your Most Valuable Asset and Your Weakest Link.

Whole books have been written about psychology and how it relates to trading. That doesn't necessarily mean they will all be helpful, but you should interpret this as a signal that the topic shouldn't be disregarded.

You must first understand the role psychology plays in trading. You must develop an understanding of your personality qualities and how they may influence your trading strategy.

A trader I know is a bad loser, and after he makes a bad deal, he has a history of going back and trying to gain those pips back, only to have even worse outcomes. But he recognizes this as a weakness, so after a bad deal, he takes a 20-minute pause before returning to trading to ensure that his emotions don't influence his trading decisions.

Second, you must strive to never stop learning. You cannot achieve a certain level and then get complacent. Every day is a learning experience in some way, so you need to be ready to pick up new abilities and spend time honing existing ones. You should stop trading the day you finish learning.

7. Recognize that Forex is Always Correct or Prepare for the Unexpected.

The Forex market is fascinating, but there is one thing that every trader needs to understand. Always plan for the unexpected and avoid getting caught up in the accomplishments of the past. Regardless of what your charts or indicators are telling you, the Forex market will occasionally behave erratically.

Whatever happens in the market, you must keep an objective perspective on your strategy and the Forex market to avoid being derailed in the long run by ripples and crashes.

Forex Trading Software

The foreign exchange market has a wide variety of tactics and systems accessible for traders, and once you start looking into your possibilities, you'll realize that the market can be both daunting and fascinating to trade because it moves so quickly.

You must study the many trading disciplines in order to start generating money from Forex trading, from comprehending the market drivers to choosing the right indicators to controlling your trading emotions.
As a Forex trader, I can attest to the fact that even if you are an expert in all facets of technical analysis, comprehend the intricacies of the market, and are knowledgeable about trading tools, none of this will matter much if you are unable to control your emotions when trading.

Trading forex will be hampered by issues like uncertainty, fear, and greed. Greed can lead to losses, fear can cloud your judgment, and emotions can make it impossible for you to successfully win at trading.

What can be done, then, to help remove emotions from the picture and allow you to trade without second-guessing your decisions? Over the years, I've come to the conclusion that it can be rather helpful to let my computer handle all of the trading and decision-making so that I can concentrate on other things.

A successful method can be used to trade the forex market automatically by handing over control of all the appropriate tactics to a robot. Profits will be taken by an automated trading system without the need for greed. It will reduce losses without allowing uncertainty and fear to govern. And finally, auto trading only uses mental energy and is unaffected by emotions. Looking over everything, this auto-trading software appears to be fine.

It is advisable that you use an automated trading robot to work for you if your forex trading isn't yielding the earnings you expected. Let's delve a little deeper and fully grasp the concept in order to achieve long-term Forex trading success.

An ambitious trader can choose between two primary ways to trade forex. Learn to trade yourself or use Forex Trading Software to let the robot handle everything. Both have achieved success in their respective fields. One is more suited for someone who works a 9 to 5 job and doesn't have time to study everything, while the other is for those who want a more leisurely and well-informed method of producing money. If correctly used, both patterns will yield positive results. Therefore, always exercise caution before investing any money in the markets.

Nowadays, there is a wide range of Forex software system trading items available that significantly reduce risk. Of course, there is little doubt that the Forex market is the most popular way to make money or support one's daily needs.

However, there are some aspects of this trading strategy that make it a dangerous game. First off, the foreign exchange market is open 24 hours a day, every day, regardless of the time zone. This implies that opportunities may present themselves at any time, including while a person is not actively trading, sleeping, or working. Because of this, forex trading is regarded as a volatile and unstable industry. Let's investigate whether there is a strategy to guarantee your profit in such hazy market conditions. Yes, if you can locate the trading Forex software system that is best for you.

Trading software assists you in making decisions based on the current state of the market without allowing emotions to get in the way of making a few good deals. Furthermore, some trading software includes money management capabilities. As a result, the software can take advantage of an opportunity anytime it presents itself. But once more, the trader using the authorized program describes the transaction limit. To be able to make profitable trades, a trader must have these fundamental skills.

Many of the Forex trading platforms on the market today offer robot-based automated trading. With the use of this technology, traders can increase their profits without turning to trading as a full-time job. With some fundamental market knowledge and the right trading tools in place, they can continue working their regular jobs or former careers while using automated trading software to make a respectable living.

It is important to note that trading in forex has never been simpler and that profitability might vary from product to product. The users of these trading software packages are able to make decisions that are not dependent on emotions but rather on calculated probability and algorithms, which is important for individuals who are just starting out in forex trading. Never will the trading software act out of fear or greed.

Users can select from a wide range of forex trading software options. Before using one of their trading philosophies, a trader must first understand the underlying theory. It is critical that you first understand who you are as a merchant. Selecting software that works well with your style of trading will be simpler for you. And you'll be much more able to achieve that. You should be able to utilize algorithmic trading to its full potential thanks to automated trade execution.

Resuming, it is ultimately up to you whether or not to purchase trading software. Do you have the time and desire to fully understand the Forex market, or would you prefer to rely on a robot once you have mastered the fundamentals? Automated trading software is not for you if you have the time and desire to become a trader for the long term or if you want to increase your wealth through trading.

After comprehending and studying the forex market, you'd want to learn the ropes and carry out everything manually. When compared with automatic trading software, which you can use if it's not your primary source of revenue. You can also begin with automated forex trading and gradually transition to manual forex trading. Whatever it is, success ultimately depends on you taking the initiative.

Get Rid of Those Bad Habits

There are several opportunities for individual traders on the forex market. For those who are willing to put forth the effort to learn, work hard, and practice patience and self-control, there is the potential to do very well financially. It is crucial for a trader learning Forex to get advice from seasoned traders to guide them along the way. Use this post to learn forex trading tips.

Once they begin to see the money coming in, people have a tendency to become avaricious. They could get overconfident as a result and make poor decisions. Panic is another emotional component that might influence decision-making and result in more bad trading judgments. Keep in mind that you must control your emotions and act in accordance with the knowledge you now possess.

Most successful Forex traders will advise you to keep some sort of journal. Finish keeping a journal in which you list your successes and failures. You can keep track of how you're doing for future reference by keeping a diary.

Don't entrust anyone other than yourself to keep an eye on your trading behavior. You are more familiar with yourself and your trading technique than anyone. You cannot rely on software to fully manage your trading. If you want to be successful at forex trading, you need to have a personal touch.

Avoid purchasing automatic Forex software that cannot be customized. You should make an effort to change your system. Your software can also be changed to better meet your unique strategy. Before you purchase your software, be sure that it is customizable.

Do you want to try your hand at forex trading? You need to have a thorough understanding of how the market functions before you start your quest. Learn about currency fluctuations and what causes swings in the currency markets. Study the foreign currencies exchanged on this market. When you are well-informed, the chances are in your favor that you will choose currencies that will appreciate in value.

Don't imagine that you can enter the Forex market and alter the entire game. Financial professionals spend a lot of time and effort learning and practicing forex trading because it is so complex. Your chances of discovering a trading strategy that performs better than these tried-and-true techniques are exceedingly slim. Conduct some studies to identify a successful strategy.

Robots should not be used in forex because they are frequently harmful to buyers. Customers hardly ever gain anything from this product; only the individuals who sell it do. Making your own trading decisions based on where you want your money to go is preferable.

Persistence is one of the few things that can help Forex traders. Every trader experiences a streak of bad luck at some point. But the difference between a successful trader and a failed trader is that the successful traders just don't give up. Keep going even when everything seems hopelessly bleak and you forget what a successful deal even looks like, and you will eventually succeed.

Anywhere online, at any moment, you can find information on forex trading. When you are sure that you are familiar with the ropes, you are more prepared for the experience. Joining a forum to communicate with others who are knowledgeable about and involved in Forex trading can be a great way to learn new things.

Why should you consider trading on the forex market above other options? You can make trades at any time because the Forex market is open every day. When it comes to forex investing, a little can go a long way. Due to both of these exceptional advantages, nearly everyone can access Forex at any given time.

Forex trading, also known as a foreign exchange strategy, was created as a way for you to profit from trading different currencies. Many people use this as a part-time or full-time means of income. Before you start purchasing and selling, you'll want to make certain that you know exactly what you're doing.

Use what you want and what you expect to choose an account and features that are appropriate for you. Recognize your limitations and be realistic.

You won't become an expert trader over night. In general, lower leverage is preferable for the majority of account types. A practice account can be used to get started because there is no danger associated with using it. Learn everything you can about forex trading.

Forex should be approached with caution because it can have a significant impact on your financial situation. People who are drawn to Forex because they want the rush of making large sums of money rapidly are mistaken. It would be more beneficial for them to give gambling a shot.

Every Forex trader needs to be aware of when to exit a position. Many times, traders see their losses increasing, but instead of cutting their losses quickly, they try to wait out the market in an effort to try to close the transaction profitably. The quickest way to lose more money is to do that.

Select a robust forex trading platform to make trading easier. There are tools available that allow you to monitor market activity and even execute trades from your smartphone. You'll achieve better flexibility and quicker reactions this way. Don't let a lack of Internet connectivity limit the number of investment alternatives available.

Make a plan and follow it. You won't succeed without a plan, so make one now. Having a plan and following it can help you resist the temptation to make decisions based on your feelings rather than your information.

You should always be thinking about risk management. Know what acceptable losses are in terms of risk management. Never go beyond your stops or limitations. You risk losing everything very soon if you become overly emotional and lose focus. Knowing when to give up and cut your losses can help you succeed.

Again, any trader who is new to the Forex market can get useful expertise and information by listening to experienced traders. Anyone looking to begin trading on the forex market should keep in mind the advice provided here. The chances are vast for traders who put in the effort and seek professional guidance.

Top FAQs About Forex Trading

With the introduction of online trading, forex trading has been rapidly expanding in popularity. Newspaper ads these days frequently tout education and currency trading as excellent ways to make money. Despite this, the world of forex remains a mystery.

Therefore, businesses are now providing top-notch trading platforms (like Metatrader 4 or MT4) that permit the usage of user-friendly Forex software to help traders improve their trading experience and ease of use. MT4 trade copier (also known as a Forex trade copier) and MT4 programming are a few of the goods and services.

Here are some queries you might have if currency trading is something you're also interested in.

The Top 5 Forex Trading FAQs

Here is a list of the top queries traders have about the forex market.

Who are the major players in the FX market, and what is it?

Any given currency can be exchanged for another currency in the forex market, also known as the foreign exchange market. For instance, the GBP and USD may be exchanged against each other, and so forth. As traders from all over the world trade their own or other currencies for others', there is constant money movement on the forex market. Another example is when multinational firms exchange currencies to cover staff wages and other costs in other nations.

Individual forex traders, also known as currency traders, who spend their time speculating on currency exchange rate fluctuations are another type of forex market participant (similar to stock traders speculating on stock prices). These rates change according to global macroeconomic conditions, money flows, and past and future predictions. During their trading, forex traders profit from even the tiniest changes in exchange rates.

Historically, banks and sizable financial institutions have been the main participants in the forex market. Individual investors are now actively participating and making investments in the forex market thanks to the rise of online trading and the development of other cutting-edge technology. Therefore, small-scale stores, brokerage houses, and individual speculators are today's key participants.

What distinguishes the forex market from other markets?

In terms of how it functions, the forex market is different from the stock market. For instance, there is no central authority or government that oversees the forex market. Thus, credit agreements between parties are a prerequisite for any forex transactions. Additionally, since there are no clearing houses for authenticating trades, there is no panel to whom one can turn in the event of a dispute.

How can I begin Forex Trading?

Start with a demo account if you're new to forex trading to learn the ropes and get some practice. Beginners can test out various trading methods with a demo account without risking any real money. Traders can use one of the numerous reputable trading systems, such as Metatrader 4 (MT4), to evaluate the market and carry out trades automatically. Effective Forex software and MT4 programming services are among the many services provided by numerous businesses. Investors who feel comfortable using demo accounts can open a trading account with a brokerage house.

How do I pick the Best Platform for Trading Forex?

The best trading platform is the one that best serves a user's demands and interests. A forex broker often provides trading platforms. Therefore, the broker you select will determine your Forex trading platform. The top trading platforms are simple to use and provide 24/7 customer support. Additionally, they have built-in market analysis that aids traders in making informed trading selections. So, new traders must first obtain a demo account to confirm the platform's suitability.

Is trading in Forex Expensive?

The broker determines how much trading in currencies will cost. While some brokers use a commission-based system, others employ a more involved strategy. Therefore, it is essential to directly question your broker about their fees, including any hidden fees, and carefully read the contract. Additionally, in order to reduce risk, traders should execute margin trades using a 20:1 leverage ratio.

Conclusion

By following these methods and learning to trade the Forex market like a professional rather than just trading it, you'll place yourself on the road to ultimate success as a successful Forex trader. 90% of all beginning traders are unable to accomplish this.

About The Author

Robert Hill has more than three decades of expertise in business-to-business, high-tech, and direct response marketing. He is a professional writer, speaker, and marketing consultant.

He shares his tried-and-true methods with self-driven, diligent people in order to assist them in achieving personal and financial independence after having achieved both.

Numerous print books, dozens of ebooks, and hundreds of articles have all been authored and published by him.

After spending more than 30 years winging the creative process, he is now devoting his life to understanding it in order to aid creative businesses and individuals think more quickly and productively (and that includes himself).

CPSIA information can be obtained
at www.ICGtesting.com
Printed in the USA
LVHW020402050523
746127LV00004B/805